DATE DUE

D1058107

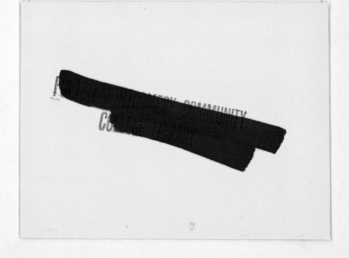

UNIVERSITY OF MINNESOTA

U. g ns i n n. # 4

Henry James

BY LEON EDEL

05880

UNIVERSITY OF MINNESOTA PRESS • MINNEAPOLIS

Printed in the United States of America at
the North Central Publishing Company, St. Paul

Library of Congress Catalog Card Number: 60-62855

third printing 1963

Distributed to high schools in the United Stattes by
McGraw-Hill Book Company, Inc.

New York   Chicago   Corte Madera, Calif.   Dallas

PUBLISHED IN GREAT BRITAIN, INDIA, AND PAKISTAN BY THE OXFORD
UNIVERSITY PRESS, LONDON, BOMBAY, AND KARACHI, AND IN
CANADA BY THOMAS ALLEN, LTD., TORONTO

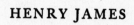

HENRY JAMES

˄ Henry James

Henry James was the "largest" literary figure to come out of America during the nineteenth and early twentieth centuries. He was not "large" as Melville is large; he did not have Melville's global vision, nor did he dream of epical landscapes. His largeness stemmed rather from the literary territories he annexed to the New World and the career he fashioned in two hemispheres. At a time when American literature was still young and certain of its writers were still sharpening their pens, Henry James crossed from the New World to the Old and was able to take his seat at the table of fiction beside George Eliot and Turgenev, Flaubert and Zola. He found the novel in English still the easy undisciplined and relaxed form it had been from its early days, and he refashioned it into a complex work of literary art. If he was junior to the fellow-craftsmen whom he joined in Europe, he achieved, in the fullness of time, a status equal to them, and in some instances he surpassed them. For he was not only a practitioner of fiction; he was one of its finest critics and theorists. It was he who gave us the terminology most useful in our time for the criticism of the novel.

Henry James wrote for fifty years; he was a prolific writer and several times glutted his own market in the magazines. Never a "best seller," as we know best sellers today, he nevertheless earned an honorable living by his pen. He was fortunate in being born into an affluent family; but from his early twenties he began to earn his own way and wholly by literary work. He was alone among major American writers in never seeking any other employment. He was devoted to his art; and his productivity did not

5

influence his meticulous style — that style by which he believed a writer gains his passport to posterity. At first his prose was fresh and clear; later it became magnificently weighted and complex in its allusiveness and imagery — and accordingly in its evocative power. His goals remained always aesthetic. He believed from the first that the artist in fiction is a historian of that part of life never found in history books: the private life that goes on behind the walls of dwellings, but which is also a part of the society in which it is lived. Literature for him was the great repository of life; and he believed that if the novel is a mirror in a roadway, it reflects not only the panorama of existence, but the countenance of the artist in the very act of experiencing the world around him.

᾿ During his five decades of creation he brought into being some twenty novels and more than one hundred tales, some of them almost of novel length. He was the first of the great psychological realists in our time, on a much more complicated and more subtly subjective level than his Russian predecessors, Turgenev, Tolstoi, and Dostoevski. In his productivity and the high level of his writing, in his insight into human motivation, and in his possession of the architectonics of fiction, he was a remarkable innovator, constantly fertile, bold, and independent — and a man with a style. R. P. Blackmur has imaged him as a sort of Shakespeare of the novel, in the power with which he brought into being, at the century's turn, with extraordinary rapidity, his three magisterial works — *The Ambassadors*, *The Wings of the Dove*, and *The Golden Bowl* — as Shakespeare set down in fast succession his three great tragedies at the turn of another century. René Wellek has spoken of James as a kind of American Goethe, Olympian in his view of literature and life, certainly in his capacity to hold both at arm's length as he analyzed and reflected upon them — upon poetry and truth, man and reality. Such a continuing reassessment of James's reputation — so recently set aside and disparaged — may bring him

6

to his proper place among the world's large literary figures, and establish him among the greatest artists of the novel.

Criticism indeed has not done sufficient justice to Henry James's uniqueness in fiction. He alone created the cosmopolitan novel in English and made of it a rich study of men, manners and morals on two continents. More significant still, he was able to treat both as comedy and as tragedy his transatlantic vision of the New World's relations to the Old. In doing this he anticipated the central fact of the twentieth century — America's assumption, among the nations of the world, of those international responsibilities from which it once isolated itself. James early recognized the drama of the confrontation of the New World and the Old — at a time when the Americans were too busy on their own expanding continent to be aware of it, and when Europe considered itself sufficiently distant to be able to ignore its transatlantic offspring, or to be interested in it essentially as the land of Fenimore Cooper's Indians or as a land to be viewed with that "certain condescension" of which Lowell complained.

In James's fiction Americans are often treated as if they still possess the innocence of Eden; and in their unawareness of evil they are shown as highly vulnerable once they venture outside their American paradise. This large drama James projected, during his later phase, as a drama of consciousness, for he had a profound sense of man's inner life. All his virtuosity was addressed, in his fiction, to discovering how to capture in words the subjective, the reflective, and even the phantasmagorial side of man.

It is because Henry James wrote so much and experimented so widely, was so complex a literary "case," that criticism has found it difficult to see him whole. In recent years, nevertheless, his authority and his vision have increasingly imposed themselves, and certain of his formulations have entered into the very texture of twentieth-century literary thought. As one of the first modern

psychological analysts in the novel his influence has been perva-
sive. Joseph Conrad, James Joyce, Virginia Woolf, Graham
Greene, Dorothy Richardson are among the many novelists who
derived technique or aesthetic ideas from the fount of Henry
James. It was no accident that even during his lifetime certain of
his fellow-novelists abroad addressed this American in their midst
as "Master."

The literary career of Henry James extended from the last days
of the American Civil War to the middle of the first World War.
He was born in New York City and belongs, in America's literary
annals, with two other sturdy children of Manhattan, Herman
Melville and Walt Whitman. The three can now be seen as dis-
tinctly urban artists: their vision was of the sea-girt city and of the
ocean; of ferries and teeming commerce, and a city-community —
as distinct from the vision of the rooted children of the orchards
and woods of Concord. Thus, where the New England writers were
more abstract and philosophical — their works still linked to the
pulpit and the sermon in spite of a disengagement from them —
the writings of the New Yorkers dealt with things more concrete
and palpable. Melville's glimpse of faraway life in the Pacific made
him forever a great cosmopolite of the spirit; and Henry James's
transatlantic life made him a cosmopolite of fact. Walt Whitman,
for all his "cosmos," dealt in concretions. All three paid their
respects to a "flowering" New England, but they represented on
their side a great urban "flowering" — a great urban impulse — in
the new American literature.

It is not surprising that James, in later years, was to speak of his
Concord predecessors as "exquisite provincials," and indeed, of
Thoreau, as being "worse than provincial — he was parochial."
He said this not in an altogether derogatory sense: he was simply
describing their limited untraveled state, their adherence to the

homely, the worldly wisdom that came out of reflection on native ground rather than out of action and life abroad. James spoke of them as would a cosmopolite for whom the Old World and the New had figured as a kind of double-landscape from the very first. For, although he was born just off Broadway, at No. 21 Washington Place, he was taken abroad when he was less than six months old. He opened his eyes of childhood upon European lawns and gardens; and one of his earliest memories was of the Napoleonic column in the Place Vendôme. Nevertheless he was returned to Manhattan when he was just learning to walk. If his eyes had first observed Europe, his feet planted themselves firmly upon American soil — that of Washington Square, within a stone's throw of where he had been born and the Square that was to furnish him with the title of one of his most popular short novels. He spent a boyhood in the streets of what was then "uptown" but what is today the lower part of Fifth Avenue. With summers in Staten Island, and trips up the Hudson, with the familiar teeming scenes of Broadway, and in a New York of muddy streets with chickens on the sidewalks and pigs rooting in the gutters, James reached the age of twelve a thorough little Manhattanite.

His grandfather had been an Irish immigrant who amassed a large fortune in Albany. His father was a religious visionary who embraced the exalted dreams of Swedenborg and Blake. His elder brother, William James, grew up to found at Harvard the first psychological laboratory in America, to write the *Principles of Psychology*, and to become America's philosopher of pragmatism. The senior Henry James had a comfortable income and was a restless wanderer. Twice during his adolescence Henry was taken to Europe, from twelve until sixteen, and again during his seventeenth year. The father gave his sons tutors and governesses, and Henry attended an assortment of schools, but his education was erratic. Much of it was carried on in European museums, galleries,

9

and parks. From the first, the future novelist had before him the two worlds: the early-forming America, in all of its indigenous rawness and with its European borrowings — and the European scene, as a series of cities, Geneva, Paris, London, and the Boulogne-sur-Mer of Thackeray, as well as the suburbs of the British metropolis.

Henry was a sensitive and shy boy; he tended to assume a quiet observer's role beside his active elder brother. He was an inveterate reader of novels; indeed it might be said that no novelist before James had had so thorough a saturation in the fiction of both sides of the Atlantic. Having learned French in his childhood, he read through shelvesful of French novels as well as the great English novelists from Richardson to the then-serialized Dickens and Thackeray. His father spoke of him as a "devourer of libraries"; for a while the parent worried about this and attempted to make his son attend a preparatory school for engineers. Henry resisted this experience as he was to resist the study of law two or three years later. He wanted to be simply "literary" and he realized this goal more rapidly than might have been expected.

On the eve of the Civil War the family returned from the third of their European journeys and settled at Newport in Rhode Island. The seventeen-year-old Henry here formed a friendship with John La Farge, the painter, his senior by several years, who guided him in his reading of French works and encouraged him to begin writing. During the early weeks of the war Henry suffered a strained back while helping to put out a fire and this "obscure hurt," as he called it in his memoirs, kept him from military service. In 1862 he registered at the Harvard Law School but soon withdrew, for he was already writing short stories and book reviews.

The earliest identified piece of fiction is an unsigned tale, "A Tragedy of Error," published in the *Continental Monthly*, a New

York magazine, in February 1864. It is a precocious tale, lurid and melodramatic, yet strangely talented. It reveals that Henry, at the threshold of his manhood, already possessed a vigorous grasp of certain storytelling techniques which were to guide him in all his work and culminate in the remarkable architecture of his final novels. His second tale dealt with life on the civilian front of the Civil War and was accepted by the *Atlantic Monthly* in 1865 when he was twenty-two. From then on the pages of this magazine were open to him. The *North American Review* and the newly founded *Nation* accepted his book reviews and when William Dean Howells began to work for the *Atlantic* he gave Henry encouragement and editorial support, recognizing at once that he had to do with a young man of extraordinary talent. Indeed by the time Henry had published half a dozen short stories a reviewer in the *Nation* spoke of him as one of the most skillful writers of fiction in America. However, from the first, the critics complained that his heroes did not lead a life of action; they tended to be self-absorbed and reflective, and the tales themselves took as their subjects problems in human behavior. The stories of this early period deal entirely with the American scene and show the leisurely existence of the well-to-do in Newport, Boston, and New York. James's models were largely French: Balzac, Mérimée, George Sand. But his writing at this time shows also an attentive reading of Hawthorne.

There is a touch of Hawthorne in "The Romance of Certain Old Clothes" (1868), first of the many ghostly tales James was to write. His most ambitious story of this period was "Poor Richard" (1867), which described a young man's helplessness in courtship when faced with rather vigorous rivals. James republished a few of these tales, much revised, in England in a series of volumes called *Stories Revived* (1885), among them "A Landscape Painter" and "A Day of Days" of 1866, "A Most Extraordinary Case" (1868), and "A Light Man" (1869). Later he disavowed all his early stories and chose to date his literary debut from the appearance of "A Passionate Pilgrim" in the *Atlantic Monthly* during 1871.

During 1869 and 1870 Henry James went abroad on his first adult journey. He was twenty-six and the experience was unforgettable. For the first time he crossed the Alps into Italy, but before doing this he renewed his old boyhood impressions of London. Here he found Charles Eliot Norton, the Harvard professor of fine arts who had published him in the *North American Review*, and through Norton met William Morris, Rossetti, and Ruskin. He also paid a call on Darwin. As he traveled, he gradually became aware of the theme that was to be central to his writings: he observed his journeying fellow-Americans in hotels and pensions, captured their sense of dislocation while trying to imbibe foreign culture; he studied particularly the itinerant American families with passive mothers and undisciplined children, and noted the absence from their lives of any standard of culture and behavior. These were the shortcomings of American innocence. On the other hand James was not blind to certain other aspects of life abroad; it is striking how often the adjective "corrupt" precedes the word "Europe" in his writings. He found in the old countries, nevertheless, a continuing spectacle of life and art. The Italian towns on their hillsides, the spires of the churches gleaming in the landscape, customs and manners bearing witness to time and tradition, served as a constant stimulus to his imagination. The galleries of Europe provided a feast for his eyes. His complaint on returning home was at one with Hawthorne: in America there was only raw nature, the forest primeval, and a broad, daylight prosperity. Eden would have been a dull place for a novelist.

While he was in England the news reached him that his beloved cousin, Minny Temple, to whom he had formed a deep if unvoiced attachment, had died. This was the climax of his "passionate pilgrimage"; and it was to be remembered in *The Portrait of a Lady* and years later in *The Wings of the Dove*. The twelve-month of wandering in England, France, and Italy — the countries in which he was to travel for the rest of his life — had set the scene for all his future. He was to remain satisfied with this terrain; he traveled neither to Spain nor to the Isles of Greece; he only briefly visited the Low Countries, and on two trips cast a hurried glance at Munich. The capitals in Jamesian geography, • extending from the New World to the Old, were Boston and New York, London, Paris, and Rome. Florence and Venice were way stations. And occasionally James explored the rural scenery of these countries. But his particular landscape was that of the humans who peopled these places and whose lives he dealt with as a part of a continuing Americano-European *comédie humaine*.

Before Henry James recognized that this was his fundamental theme, he made a serious attempt to discover what he could accomplish as a writer within the United States. Twice between 1870 and 1875 — first in Boston and then in New York — he sought systematically to gain a livelihood by the writing of fugitive journalism and fiction within the American scene. In Boston he wrote a short novel entitled *Watch and Ward*. For a brief moment he entertained the common fantasy of novitiates in fiction that this would be a Great American Novel: even the supersubtle James allowed himself this cliché-dream of overnight fame and power. Set in Boston and its suburbs, the novel told of a wealthy young man who adopts an orphan and rears her in the hope she will some day become his wife. The strange thing about this novel was James's failure to paint any background; he became fascinated by the relationships between the orphan, her guardian, her suitors; but the story might have taken place anywhere. Nevertheless in the book may be found an early sketching out of some of the material he would use with finished art in *The Portrait of a Lady*.

More important, at this time, was James's writing of "A Passionate Pilgrim," the only early tale he was willing, at the end of his life, to reprint. In it there is the rhapsodic note of James's rediscovery of Europe and the tale has all the ingredients of James's later "international" stories: the narrator, discovering Europe, infatuated with the things of the Old World; the contrast of American cultural bareness with the old traditions and manners of Europe and at the same time the awareness of the New World's egalitarianism, for if the American protagonist dies in England, there is an Englishman at the end of the story who goes forth with new hope to replace him in America.

During his stay in Boston James continued to write book reviews; and he tried his hand at art criticism. Early in 1875 he went to New York, spending the winter there, but found it artistically — and financially — unremunerative. Between these brief "sieges" of Boston and New York he made another journey to Europe, spending in particular a winter in Rome (1872–73) where he met many American artists and closely observed the life of the long-established American colony on the banks of the Tiber. Out of this experience came his first important novel: *Roderick Hudson*. In substance and setting it seems to take up where Hawthorne left off in *The Marble Faun*. Hawthorne attempted a characteristic "romance," reworking, in terms of the real and the mystical, the Puritan struggle between guilt and goodness in a Roman setting. James, on the other hand, wrote a novel romantic in theme — that of an American artist destroyed by his passion for a beautiful woman — yet realistic in its painting of the American art expatriates in the Holy City. On a deeper level *Roderick Hudson* reflects the conflicts experienced by Henry James at this time in his search to discover what it meant to be an American, and an artist, at this moment of history. If the novel did not find the answer, it at any rate stated the problem and weighed the possibilities. Written in a clear and highly readable style, it suffered from the excesses of first novels: the author was trying to say too much, to cram too many future novels into this one. Yet it is a work of great charm and feeling; compared with the novels being published in America at the time, it is indeed an extraordinary performance.

The novel was completed in New York in 1875 and ran through twelve installments in the *Atlantic Monthly*. With it James established the pattern by which he was to earn his living for the next forty years — that of publishing a serial in a magazine and thereby assuring himself of a steady monthly income, and augmenting this by the writing of articles, reviews, and tales. It was clear to him now that he could expatriate himself without difficulty. He could live more cheaply in Europe, and make money by his travel articles; he would find the material for his fiction and have the leisure in which to write it. By 1875 Henry had devoted a full decade to periodical publication; and now he made a substantial debut between book covers: in that year appeared *A Passionate Pilgrim and Other Tales*; a collection of travel articles, *Transatlantic Sketches*; and the novel *Roderick Hudson*. From this time on he was to publish a book or more every year — drawing upon the great backlog of his periodical writings, which he never exhausted, to make up the volumes of tales, criticism, and travel that came out at the same time as his novels.

In the autumn of 1875 he settled in Paris and one of his first acts was to call upon the Russian novelist Ivan Turgenev. James had greatly admired his work and he found in this older writer a congenial mentor. If from Balzac James had learned how to set a scene and launch a drama, and from Hawthorne how to suffuse the

LEON EDEL

drama with charm, and from George Eliot the value of endowing his story with intellectual illumination, he learned his most important lesson of all from Turgenev. This was to make his novel flow from his personages. The Russian writer provided James with the concept of the "organic" novel; he helped James to see that the novel need not be a haphazard story, but one in which characters live out their natures. This might be called "psychological determinism," and James was to become perhaps the greatest (and often misunderstood) exponent of it in his work. He was one of the rare writers of fiction to grasp the psychological truth that an action properly derives from a character, that a novel creates the greatest illusion of truth when it grows out of a personage's observations and perceptions. This is why, in James, we find an insistence upon the fundamental truths of human behavior, rather than the cheerful coloring of these truths indulged in by so many of his contemporaries. Like Turgenev and the other Russian novelists — but at an opposite emotional pole — James concerned himself with character above all else, and with people in relation to one another. Unlike the characters in Russian novels, James's personages tended to subordinate their emotions and passions to their intellect; but with extraordinary subtlety James could show the force of passion and emotion beneath the intellectual façade.

Turgenev took James to meet Flaubert; and in Flaubert's apartment, high in the rue du Faubourg St. Honoré, the American made friends with Zola, Edmond de Goncourt, Daudet, Maupassant. Later he was to know Loti, Coppée, and Bourget, who became a particularly close friend. If he had found the men of Concord to be "exquisite provincials," he felt that these Parisians lived also within narrow horizons. He felt indeed, and understandably, that he was more cosmopolitan and possessed wider experience of the world than they did, if less experience of an immediate physical environment. He ruefully remarked in a letter home that he could talk French to them but they, in their insularity, knew not a word of English.

A year in Paris sufficed. In December of 1876 Henry James crossed the channel and settled in the heart of London, a few blocks from Piccadilly Circus; and little more than a twelvemonth later he was famous both in America and England as the author of "Daisy Miller."

The career of Henry James has been divided, for convenience, by most critics into three "periods" and these were once humorously characterized by a British writer as falling (by dynastic arrangement) into those of "James I, James II, and the Old Pretender." The "Old Pretender" was an allusion to James's elaborate manner in his old age, his involuted sentences, his search for precision of statement at the expense of the patience of his listeners. A closer examination of the sequence of his works gives to his first period a distinctive unity; it is the period of his apprenticeship and his success, his discovery of his great cosmopolitan subject and his exploitation of it. It may be said to end with the triumphant writing of *The Portrait of a Lady*, long planned — and brought to completion according to plan. The second period has often been spoken of as the period of James's "social" novels; but it would be more exact to see this period as falling, in itself, into three acts: the abandoning for the time being of the "international" theme and the writing of three long novels in the naturalist mode; then the abandoning of fiction for five years of writing for the stage; in 1895 the return to the novel, followed by half a dozen years of experimental writing in which James assimilated the techniques derived from the theater. Out of these experiments emerged the third period, which — far from being that of an Old Pretender — has been more accurately described as "the major phase," certainly "major" in terms of its influence upon the twentieth-century novel. During this final phase James wrote, within a four-year period, the three novels by which he makes his greatest claim on posterity.

The first period extended from 1865 to 1882, and it is symbolized by the tale of "Daisy Miller" — the "ultimately most prosperous child of my invention," James called her many years later. During his lifetime his reputation was to rest largely upon his "studies" of young American girls encountering Europe, and Daisy became their prototype. His stories of American families touring in the Old World as if it were a painful duty rather than a civilized pleasure were famous and much discussed. Like Hawthorne's young heroes, these Americans have to discover that the world is not as innocent as it seems, and that behind the smiling façades of castles and picturesque ruins lurk centuries of wrongdoing and the dark and evil things of the human spirit. "Daisy Miller" dramatized this on a level of comedy and pathos: the tale of the young and radiant Daisy, with the dew of her homeland still freshly sprinkled over her, arriving in Rome and never realizing for a moment that European life and European standards may be different from those she has known in Schenectady, N.Y. What she deems to be a pleasant flirtation with a friendly Italian is viewed by Europeans, and even more, by Europeanized Americans, with deadly seriousness. Daisy knows no evil and is unable to think it; she cannot comprehend why her behavior, which seems harmless enough to her, should be the cause of so much social anxiety. As James himself put it: "The whole idea of the story is the little tragedy of a light, thin, natural, unsuspecting creature being sacrificed as it were to a social rumpus that went on quite over her head and to which she stood in no measurable relation. To deepen the effect, I have made it go over her mother's head as well."

The story indeed gained its power from the portraits of the wholly passive mother and the undisciplined young brother; the

picture of an upper-middle-class family, the permissive and indul-
gent parents wholly subjugated by their children, transported to
a foreign environment where the parents are helpless and ignorant
and the children run wild. The drama is heightened by the skill
with which James shows this family through the sophisticated
eyes of an American expatriate who feels he has lost touch with
his native land. His failure to understand the "new" American
girl, represented by Daisy, in the end only accentuates her sense
of isolation; the fresh Daisy can only wither and die.

In *Roderick Hudson* James had portrayed the American artist,
going abroad to find the schooling and traditions of art not available to him in his homeland. In *The American* of two years later,
his "easiest" and most romantic novel, he had drawn a picture of
a businessman possessing great charm of character and the candor
of a trusting and innocent nature, seeking to win for himself a
wife in the French aristocracy. The novel is a mixture of melo-
drama and romance, yet it dramatizes most clearly the irony James
was seeking to express to his readers. For Christopher Newman,
bearing the name of Columbus, represents one type of new man
from the New World, who has strayed among the nobles of the
Old. They are corrupt. They want to make use of him and his
wealth. They also have complete contempt for him. The American
has his chance for revenge. But he throws it away with the remark
that two wrongs do not make a right; he thereby reveals himself
more noble than the nobles, and more the Christian gentleman.
The novel ends in a splendid passage of muted emotion as Newman walks away from the bleak Paris street in which his love is
immured in her convent, and hears the "far-away bells chiming
off into space at long intervals, the big bronze syllables of the
Word." Revenge, he meditates, is not his "game."

With the success of "Daisy Miller" James promptly recognized
that the public liked his Americano-European stories and particu-

larly his tales of international marriages and of bright young
American girls discovering Europe. "The Last of the Valerii,"
"Madame de Mauves," "Four Meetings," and "Daisy Miller" itself had fully attested to this. And now he began to play out his
themes in all their variations — stories of the self-made girl, who
arranges life for her fiancé so she may make a splendid marriage;
stories of English noblewomen who marry Americans but despise
them; and of Americans unable to grasp the guile and duplicity
of certain kinds of Europeans. His tales were clever, witty, charm-
ing; he was in all the magazines and editors asked for more —
which he always gave them; it seems now, when one looks over
the long list of his "international" productions, as if he wrote with
both hands. When London laughed too heartily over Daisy and
her young brother, James replied by writing a tale in which
Americans could laugh at the smugness and fatuity of Britons
visiting America ("An International Episode"). But he was play-
ing upon national sensitivities: the Americans and English
enjoyed laughing at each other; they did not care to laugh at
themselves.

In his late prefaces James spoke of his "Americano-European
legend," and showed how clearly he had envisaged his international dramas. What his stories had represented, he said, was a
record of the American "state of innocence," that of the Americans
being "almost incredibly *unaware of life* — as the old European
order expressed life," and what he had studied was "their more or
less stranded helplessness" abroad. And he went on: "Conscious
of so few things in the world, these unprecedented creatures were
least of all conscious of deficiencies and dangers; so that, the grace
of youth and innocence and freshness aiding, their negatives were
converted and became in certain relations lively positives and
values." Out of their experience he fashioned the comedy and
pathos and beauty of their state. His long observation of traveling

20

Americans, his thorough knowledge of the American character, his saturation in European life, had given him his data. He was artist enough to make of it splendid literary capital. But if he treated it in his shorter tales on a level of wit and comedy — and in a comic spirit which has never been sufficiently praised — he found in it also larger and more tragic implications. These he embodied in the novel which marked the end of this phase — *The Portrait of a Lady*.

It was planned for almost a decade. To write it, James produced in fast succession three short novels and a nonfictional work — his *Hawthorne* — earning in this way the funds needed to pursue his big novel at leisure. During the next fifteen months his works literally tumbled from the presses in England and America. *The Europeans* came out in October 1878; "Daisy Miller" and two other tales, in a two-volume edition, appeared in February 1879; in October of the same year he issued another collection of tales, and in December there came out, within two days of each other, the short novel *Confidence* and the *Hawthorne*. By this time James had also completed the last of this group, *Washington Square*, which was published during 1880 while he was preparing the first installments of *The Portrait of a Lady*.

The *Hawthorne* was written at the request of John Morley for the English Men of Letters Series. It is a finished piece of work, the tribute of one American genius to another. The argument of the book was that America had been bare of society and history when Hawthorne came upon the scene; having no rich social fabric such as English novelists could draw upon, he tissued his work out of the haunted Puritan history of New England. In depicting the America of Hawthorne's time, and in describing certain institutions "absent" from American life, James touched American editorial sensitivities. "In the United States, in those days, there were no great things to look out at (save forests and rivers); life was not in the least spectacular; society was not brilliant; the country was given up to a great material prosperity, a homely bourgeois activity, a diffusion of primary education and the common luxuries." Sentences such as this one, while accurate enough, seemed to certain of his readers depreciatory. Perhaps James used the word "provincial" too many times. Perhaps his easy cosmopolitanism was translated as condescension. A formulation such as "in the light, fresh American air, unthickened by customs and institutions" invited challenge. And when James described the materials available to the English novelist of manners — court, church, society, peerage, and so forth — he was held to be making invidious and undemocratic comparisons. His book set off a sharp flurry in the American press, and from this time on there was formed the legend that James was an expatriate who mocked his countrymen and exalted Europe at the expense of America.

Today we can see the *Hawthorne* for what it is: a finely sketched picture of Hawthorne's Salem and Concord, and a profoundly accurate critique of his work. The tone and the style of the book is felicitous at every turn. It contains a large measure of devotion to New England and its traditions, and its picture of Brook Farm and the Transcendentalists is drawn from intimate and affection- ate sources. But there was no denying that the book served equally to veil James's defense of his own work, and the shortcomings of *his* America — for the kind of novelist he was and sought to be.

The three short novels were thrown off in a happy and spon- taneous vein. They represent James at his most gifted "profes- sionalism." The least important was a novel called *Confidence*, which is talented hack work, a minor comedy of manners. The most important, *Washington Square*, set in New York, was the story of a plain girl who lived in a big house in the Square with her wealthy father, but who was prevented by him from having the shoddy lover she wanted to marry. This novel, written as if it were a piece of naturalism by the Goncourts or a neo-Balzacian *Eugénie Grandet,* has long been a favorite with readers of James and won him wide popularity long after his death when it was dramatized and cinematized as *The Heiress.* James always regarded it as a trifling work, stale and flat and without the richer experimental values of his best narratives. His third potboiler was *The Europeans,* written in response to an appeal from William Dean Howells that he give the *Atlantic Monthly* a story less sober and tragic than *Roderick* and more cheerful than *The American.* To accomplish this James reversed his "international" situation; instead of showing Americans abroad, he brought back to Boston two Americans who had lived in Europe for so long that they had little knowledge of their own country. How they fare among a group of rigid New Englanders was the situation out of which James's comedy of *The Europeans* grew. Boston readers were not amused. Today, however, the story reads as one of the brightest and most humorous of the novelist's inventions.

Now he could finally set to work on *The Portrait of a Lady.* He took a vacation in Italy and got the book under way, carefully revising each section. He had succeeded in selling it to *Macmillan's* magazine in London as well as to the *Atlantic* and this brought him a substantial income during the period of serialization. More important still, it firmly established him before a public on both sides of the ocean. The novel was his largest and most carefully wrought canvas to date; and if his career had ended after producing it he would still rank as a major figure in the history of American fiction. As it was, he was to go on to even greater achievements during the next thirty years.

The Portrait of a Lady was the third in James's group of fictional American expatriations; he had "done" the artist in Rome and the businessman in Paris. Now he brought Isabel Archer, the young girl from Albany, to England, and placed her among her

LEON EDEL

suitors in the Old World. She, too, is an heiress; she is given the
freedom for which she romantically strives. She is an idealistic and
intelligent girl, not the flirtatious hunting-for-a-husband girl
James had pictured in Daisy Miller or Pandora Day. And the
drama in which she becomes involved resides in the choice which
she thinks she "freely" makes. Having the opportunity to marry a
British Lord, she shrinks from being drawn into the life of the
nobility, with its rituals and its responsibilities; she shrinks equally
from marrying an intense and overinsistent, but upright, American. Neither marriage, she feels, would leave her free. When she
makes her choice, it is to marry the one man who in the end limits
her freedom most — an American dilettante, fastidious and fussy,
who "collects" her — and her money — as he collects his *objets
d'art*. But if Isabel has been the victim of her own generous nature
and her romantic illusions, she has also been the victim of a carefully laid plot: the man she marries has a daughter by a former
mistress, Madame Merle, who has become Isabel's best friend; and
it is through Madame Merle's connivance that the heiress has been
steered into the orbit of the dilettante that she may assure, by her
fortune, the future of the child.

This melodramatic underpinning of the story is handled with
the novelist's characteristic realism. He knew that he could make
the reader swallow almost any story if his people were truly drawn;
and the series of portraits of the characters surrounding Isabel —
no less than Isabel herself — give the novel its remarkable force
and intensity. Few "psychological" villains have ever been
sketched with greater power than Gilbert Osmond, the pretentious
and cynical husband; and his scheming yet sympathetic mistress,
Madame Merle, is one of James's most completely realized characters. The novel shows step by step how the unconventional and
"free" Isabel is "ground in the very mill of the conventional." The
"portrait" of the lady — her private history, her illusions and her

24

disillusionment — is in essence a psychological portrait. Isabel confronts her destiny with courage and determination: but James shows us that behind this bold free attitude there are fears and uncertainties. What is dramatized in the novel is New World romanticism foundering upon hard realities long known to the Old World. The novel's success lies in its brilliant projection of the American girl, the delineation of her character, and the establishment of a *tone*: this is achieved in great part by a remarkable narrative rhythm, an unfailing sense of narrative movement.

When the novel was nearing its end in the magazines, Henry returned to America. He was received in Boston, New York, and Washington as the successful if often criticized author who had made a reputation for himself abroad. His mother died during his stay in America; and he had barely returned to England when he was summoned back to Boston, to the deathbed of his father. He was named executor, and after arranging for the division of the family property, he once more crossed the Atlantic. This time he was to remain abroad for twenty years. He inherited a modest income, but he was making his way so successfully that he turned this over to his sister, and continued to live by his pen.

The novelist now entered upon the second period of his writings. It was marked by his decision to attempt new subjects. He was tired of the "international" theme and he felt that he had exhausted it. With extraordinary energy he wrote two long novels during the next three years — *The Bostonians* and *The Princess Casamassima*. The American novel dealt with New England reformers; the *Princess* with another and more dangerous kind of reformer, the European anarchists. These novels are, in a sense, tales of two cities — Boston and London. They are brilliantly "social" in their painting of certain scenes of urban life and they are a calculated attempt by James to write a "naturalistic" novel.

LEON EDEL

A visit to Paris in 1884 and long talks with Zola, Edmond de Goncourt, and Daudet had deeply impressed him. James failed this time, however, to take the measure of his public: it was awaiting more tales from him about helpless and bright Americans in Europe, and wandering foreigners in the United States (such as those described in "The Point of View"). Instead James offered his readers a realistic and minutely painted picture of Bostonian suffragettes and another of London radicals; this was the kind of novel which was not to gain a firm hold until the Edwardian period, and which in America would have as its foremost exponents Norris and later Dreiser. In attempting to place the American novel into the stream of the Zolaesque Continental fiction, James alienated his limited but appreciative public. The novels were flat failures.

He made one more attempt. This time he wrote of the world of art and tried to record the problems confronting a young politician-painter and an actress. *The Tragic Muse* ran for many months in the *Atlantic Monthly*, yet it had small success with its readers for all the brilliancy of its writing. James, with his experimental attitude toward the novel, had done more than switch from his main theme: he had tried "naturalism" but he was an incomplete "naturalist" — naturalism relying on literalism and the portrayal of primitive passion and violence. What James created was a series of subtle studies of individuals caught in forces and movements beyond their control, undone by conflicts between their temperaments and their environment. James's "determinism" was essentially psychological, where Zola's was physical. *The Princess Casamassima* anticipated by five decades the major theme of the twentieth century — the young man who seeks to overthrow the very society in which he in reality also seeks acceptance.

While he was writing these novels he continued to turn out a brilliant series of tales; some of them were of such length that by

26

current measurement they are counted as short novels. On the eve of his writing of *The Tragic Muse* he set down his story of "The Aspern Papers" — a narrative masterpiece in its evocation of a dying Venice and a dying old lady trying to keep from a privacy-invading age the love letters written to her more than half a century before by a great poet. The story moves with the rhythmic pace and tension of a superb mystery story; and the double climax — the unmasking of the "publishing scoundrel" and the proposal made to him by the middle-aged niece, that he marry her and receive the Aspern papers as a "dowry" — give this tale the high drama reflected in the extraordinary success of Sir Michael Redgrave's play version. Grave matters are treated with the lightest of touch and with a deep humanity. Between the lines of "The Aspern Papers" James is saying that an artist's life should be preserved from prying hands, that he should be read in his work alone. Yet James is also, ambivalently, on the side of the biographer who seeks the human elements in the artist's work. He based the tale on a brief anecdote of a Boston collector who had taken rooms in the Florentine home of Claire Clairmont, Byron's mistress, in the hope of finding Shelley and Byron relics. Out of this hint, and out of his own deep love of Venice, James fashioned a narrative that belongs to the golden age of storytelling.

In 1889 Henry James faced the fact that if he had had great success a decade earlier, he was now a distinguished man of letters with several distinct public failures on his hands. He knew that he was a finer artist than ever; he had, as always, a sense of his destiny; but he had written three big novels which we now know were destined for posterity rather than for his time. The income from his writings had been reduced to a low point; vigorous measures were necessary. He accordingly sought to revive his fortunes by turning to the theater. During the next five years, from 1890 to 1895, he wrote seven plays. Two of them reached the stage: a •

dramatization of *The American* which had a modest run, and *Guy Domville*, a carefully written costume play, produced in 1895 by the popular London manager George Alexander. This was booed by an ill-tempered audience which vented its anger on James himself, when he came out to take a bow on his first night. Repudiated once again by his public, and this time in an open and violent fashion, James turned his back on the theater and resumed his writing of fiction.

In a sense he turned his back on his public altogether. He withdrew from London, after years of city life, living first in a rented house, and later purchasing Lamb House, in Rye, Sussex, at the top of a winding cobbled street in that picturesque coastal town. It was an old house, and had a walled garden. This became his permanent abode, although he later kept rooms at the Reform Club and in the end had a flat in Cheyne Walk. It was in Lamb House that his final works were written, and here that he partially resolved the deep feeling of frustration and failure engendered by public indifference to his art. He had been writing shorter tales on the margin of his unsuccessful novels and during his nervous adventures in the theater. He was at the top of his narrative power just before plunging into the theater, as "The Aspern Papers" of 1887 and the delicately conceived "The Pupil" of 1891 show. Now he wrote a series of tales which are patently autobiographical, dealing in wry fashion with writers who know they have greatness in their pen but who cannot somehow meet the simple and unsubtle requirements of readers and critics. Between the failure of *Guy Domville* and the turn of the century the fictions of Henry James show him experimenting at every turn, but also selecting themes reflecting the crisis of his career: the troubled sense that he was a "lost" author, unwanted by an indifferent and illiterate world.

When he was not writing his parables about unsuccessful writers he wrote ghostly tales; indeed most of his tales in this form belong to this haunted period. And it was between 1895 and 1900 that he set down his series of stories of ravaged childhood and adolescence, in reality a reworking of his theme of innocence in a corrupting world.

The most celebrated in this group, which combines both the theme of tormented childhood and the ghostly element, is "The Turn of the Screw." James himself dismissed it as trivial: he told Howells it was a "down-on-all-fours pot-boiler." Nevertheless it promptly captured the imagination of his readers and has held it ever since. No work of James's has, indeed, stirred up more argument or provoked more insistent claims by critics, each insisting on his particular interpretation. The truth is that every reader can supply his own reading. James revealed on more than one occasion how he deliberately sought ambiguity so that his reader would imagine his own "horror" — on the theory that a nightmare is most frightening to the person who dreams it. In this fashion he established the ground for an unusual collaboration between author and reader. The haunted governess is the narrator, but she supplies few tangible "facts," and the reader is placed in the difficult position of having to determine, from the story she tells — and the way she tells it — how reliable a witness she is. James called this "a trap for the unwary." Most readers, caught up in the movement of the narrative, understandably take the governess's account in good faith. But if the reader begins to study her testimony he notices that it does not always hang together, and that the very language she uses is filled with imagery which reveals her own terror in the midst of her apparent composure.

By the governess's own account the children never see the ghosts which are haunting her. The reader, on his side, consciously or unconsciously, is sensitized to one of two horrors, or indeed to both: he may participate in the governess's terror that the children are exposed to damnation, or be terrified himself at the children's being exposed to such an anxiety-ridden governess. Out of such shadowings, such "gleams and glooms," as James called them, the novelist created one of the most profoundly evocative stories ever written. "The Turn of the Screw" illustrates James's matured theory of the ghostly tale. Awe and mystery, he held, do not hinge on the crime and the cadaver, the dark castle, chains, blood, secret trapdoors, and frankensteins walking at midnight. James's ghosts walk mostly in broad daylight. He creates his eerie atmosphere by having the unusual occur on the margin of the usual. In this way the horror is greatly intensified. What James added to the ghostly tale, in reality, were a series of acute studies of forms of human anxiety—of the capacity of humans to scare themselves with phantoms of their own creation.

Among his other stories of troubled childhood were *What Maisie Knew*, the story of a little girl who lives alternately with each of her divorced parents and is flung from one to the other as if she were a tennis ball, and how she tries, in the process, to fathom the strange moral world in which she sees them living; "In the Cage," the tale of a girl in late adolescence, who works in a branch post office and seeks to construct in her imagination the fashionable world whose telegrams pass through her hands; and *The Awkward Age*, a novel concerned with the female adolescent who reaches the time when she can put up her hair and join her elders in the drawing room. A kind of childish curiosity is at the center of these stories, curiosity about sex and manners and the ways of the adult world. And James conveys in them the bewilderment—and often the terror—of the young plastic consciousness trying to come to terms with a world that it can experience but cannot wholly comprehend. If the theme of these stories reflects a regression by James to his own bewildered early state when *he* had tried to fathom the adult world (and was now trying again, since it had rejected him), they also show the delicate probing by a subtle artist of the sexual mores of Victorian England.

The technical innovations in these tales are perhaps even more important than their themes: for James was led to explore methods of narration which would accurately render the consciousness of childhood *in terms of its own unawareness.* To do this he resorted increasingly to the lessons he had learned in the theater: revelation of action through scene, use of dialogue as narration, removal of the omniscient author from his role as informer and commentator. This meant also imposing upon the reader the burden of ferreting out for himself what is happening in the story. In a sense it converts the reader into an author, it places him at the author's window in the "house of fiction." Few readers were willing during James's lifetime to accept the responsibility he asked them to assume, or yield that "attention of perusal" which he demanded. His discovery of the possibilities of merging stagecraft with fictional method is one of the great moments of revelation in his notebooks, in which he recorded *"the singular value for a narrative plan* of the . . . divine principle of the Scenario . . . this exquisite truth that what I call the divine principle in question is a key that . . . fits the complicated chambers of *both* the dramatic and narrative lock."

That James fully discovered this "singular value" may be discerned in the final period of his career, those years from 1900 to the first World War which are now spoken of as constituting his "major phase." The three large novels which Henry James wrote between 1900 and 1904 — in which he returned to his "international" subjects and this time on a grandiose scale — can be understood only in the light of the techniques of James's maturity. At the end, form and substance coalesced to give us the psychological drama of James's highest comedy, *The Ambassadors*, the brooding tragedy of *The Wings of the Dove*, and what might be called James's supreme novel of manners, *The Golden Bowl*.

The Ambassadors, published in 1903 but written between 1899 and 1901, exemplified both James's use of "point of view" (that is, the telling of the story through various angles of vision) and his method of alternation of scene. By the "point of view" method James was able to make the reader feel himself at one with the given character, and impart to him only as much of the story as that character perceives at any given moment; by alternating scenic action with his narrative of the reflective and analytic side of his personages, James created a novel unique in the history of fiction. His "ambassador" is a middle-aged New Englander who discovers how little he has been emotionally awake, because of the inhibitions of his youth and those of his environment; he finds himself balancing the rigidities of New England against the laxities of Paris, without altogether being able to shake off his own New England conscience. But he at least has been opened up to experience and has gained insight into himself. The "envoys" of *The Ambassadors* are sent out at various times to bring home American lingerers in Paris, including the original "ambassador" himself. At the core of the novel is James's mature belief that life is a process of *seeing*, and through awareness the attaining of understanding; that if man is a creature with a predetermined heredity and a molding environment, he still can cherish the "illusion of freedom." He should, therefore, James holds, make the most of this illusion.

Written in the high style of James's late years, *The Ambassadors* represents the novel form carried to a level of extraordinary "art": mere storytelling has given way to intricate effects, as on a stage. There is no scene in James more brilliantly realized than that in which Lambert Strether, thinking of an old painting of the French countryside he had once looked at in Boston, wanders into the

Parisian suburbs and finds himself, as it were, inside the frame of that painting and walking about in its landscape.

Technique is also the key to *The Wings of the Dove*, published a year before *The Ambassadors* although written immediately after that novel. It clearly exemplifies the way in which James insisted that his subject dictate his structure and why he believed he could thus achieve an "organic" novel. Wishing to write the story of a doomed girl (the disease is not specified), he told himself that fiction cannot concern itself with dying, but is concerned wholly with the act of living; and so he arranged the scenic structure of the book to keep the picture of Milly Theale's dying state from the reader save at certain moments when she affirms her will to live. The novel focuses rather on the personages around her, and on the cruel plot of her friends to supply her with a "lover" who will inherit her money and thus be free, after her death, to make the marriage he wishes. This is one of the strangest variants ever introduced into the old love triangle and James rigorously adhered to his plan: the "big" scenes, those in which the dying heroine is involved, are never written. They would have turned the novel into mere pathos. The characters hear about the events afterwards; they have occurred off-stage, as in classical tragedies. And James realizes the artistic unity of his work not only in his study of a passive young man in the hands of a fascinating and power-driven woman, but in the way in which, in the end, the dead Milly, "the dove," has changed the course of the lives of all his characters.

In a remarkable way *The Ambassadors* and *The Wings of the Dove* were an elaborate rewriting, in terms of his late maturity, of *The American* and *The Portrait of a Lady*, a weaving out of old materials of a new and complex fabric within the large vision the novelist had finally achieved of the Western world — its greatness and its glory, its corruption and its decay. James wrote out of a

LEON EDEL

charged consciousness and, as he said of Shakespeare, "out of the history of his soul and the direct exposure of his sensibility." In doing this he bethought himself of "our towering idol" — the man who had tried to write the history of the world into the France of his day, Balzac, saluted by James as "the master of us all."

Balzac had tried to create certain novels which would serve also as "philosophical studies" within the frame of his "human comedy." They had been rather poor novels, but James had looked at them attentively. And there is an implied homage to them, or to their intention, in these late works. Thus James named the hero of *The Ambassadors* Lewis Lambert Strether, after Balzac's *Louis Lambert*. To be sure, Strether himself remarks that Balzac's novel "is an awfully bad one" — but James nevertheless makes his, like Balzac's, the story of an education. There is perhaps a more profound relationship between *The Wings of the Dove* and another of the *études philosophiques*, Balzac's Swedenborgian novel *Séraphita* (which, in our time, fascinated Yeats). A great Christian awareness pervades both the *Wings* and *Séraphita*: and both tell of a young woman who enacts the sacrifice of Christ. Séraphita says "there are two ways of dying — to some death means victory, to some it is defeat" — and Milly's great moral triumph is in making of her death a victory and a sacrifice. Balzac's work is, however, mystical whereas James's is grounded in the human stuff of nobility and betrayal, grandeur and defeat. To Balzac James may be said to be indebted for the symbolism of his novel — in both works we seem to hear a beating of great angelic wings, and the heroines are found perched on the edge of great abysses, surveying the precipices and terrors of the life they are to leave. Séraphita wishes she had "wings to cover you withal" and "the wings of the dove" in James's book in the end enfold those who sought to betray her. In these novels James created dramas of man, within the large social organisms man has shaped for himself, and within the ideas by

34

which he reared his churches and his civilization. Perhaps for this reason, certain critics have tried to read allegories into them, over-looking the fact that James rejected this form of writing and held himself a realist concerned with things visible and palpable. His tradition was not that of the Divine Comedy, but of the *comédie humaine*.

If these two major works of the final phase reached back to earlier fictions, James's ultimate novel, *The Golden Bowl*, reveals him breaking new ground and finding a resolution to questions left unresolved in his other novels. He chooses a triangle — husband, wife, mistress — but the twist this time is that he marries off the mistress to the father of the wife, makes her the stepmother of the betrayed heroine. A subject as "adulterine" as this James had wanted to treat for many years, complaining that the American "family" magazines made him write at the level of adolescents. But *The Golden Bowl* was not serialized, and he was free to handle his subject without any reservations. The novel is, for once, the record of an innocent American girl who really does grow up: in the end she has not only won back her husband, but has emerged from her all-but-fatal attachment to her father. She sends the father back to America with his young wife and remains in Europe to work out her own future; her marriage is restored and her relationship with her husband "reconstructed" on the firm founda-tion of maturity: the immaturities had been her own. This time in James, the marriages are not failures: the alliances between Europeans and Americans are consummated and made strong and durable, and possessed of a future. To say this is but to give the bald elements of a remarkable work, rich in James's most elaborate metaphors. His exploration of the consciousness of the Italian Prince and his American Princess is subtle — she at first as innocent and as ignorant as Isabel Archer; he an aristocrat, taking life as it comes, and ready to ignore his wife if she fails to live up to his high sophistication. She learns actively to *see*; and through this awareness triumphs.

These three novels would seem to be accomplishment enough for any writer; but James, asserting always that he was a slow and poor "producer," also put forth during this time the series of brilliant stories contained in volumes titled *The Soft Side*, *The Better Sort*, and *The Finer Grain*. Perhaps the most famous of these tales, certainly the most widely read in recent years, is "The Beast in the Jungle," whose forty-odd pages encompass the entire life of an individual — an individual so wrapped in his own egotism that his eyes are sealed to the real experiences of life. He knows only the dark jungle of his own existence. The beast that waits to spring upon him is the emptiness of his life, his failure to understand and to love. As a parable against the blindness of self, and as a picture of the darkness *within*, this story belongs with Conrad's "Heart of Darkness" and T. S. Eliot's "The Hollow Men."

If, at the end of *The Golden Bowl*, Henry James sent Adam Verver and Charlotte, his wife, back to America, it was perhaps because he was about to return himself. He had been away during all his middle years — from his fortieth to his sixtieth year. He was curious, he wanted to take a look at his past. America received him with enthusiasm; he was invited to lecture and to write his impressions; he traveled to the south for the first time and he realized a long-cherished dream when he crossed the continent and saw California. Although he returned to England with a sigh of relief, after a strenuous year, it was with the sense that he had captured the whole new aspect of the United States. His book *The American Scene* is one of his great prose works: with the brush of an impressionist painter he restlessly analyzes things as they were, and as they had become; he had known old New York and now confronted the skyscrapers; he had known a tight parochial

Boston; he now saw a sprawling city. Only Concord seemed much the same, and he wondered whether it had not been in its time a sort of "American Weimar." He revisited it with warm memory of Emerson. He revisited also the family plot in the Cambridge cemetery and wrote into his notebook a lyrical passage that expressed all the felt intensity of that experience. What bothered him about America was that so booming a civilization, capable of the greatest things, was addressed so markedly to material ends. This is the repeated refrain of *The American Scene*.

While in the United States he reached an agreement with his publisher to assemble his novels and tales into a definitive edition. For three years after his return to Lamb House he labored on this task, thinking of Balzac and the way in which the French novelist had harmonized his stories and novels and created categories for them in his *comédie humaine*. The "New York Edition," as James titled it, was rigorously selective. It emphasized the cosmopolitan character of his work, and he selected for inclusion his "international" and psychological stories. He left out those novels and tales which had America for a setting, apparently planning to add these, as a separate group, at some later time. All his early works were carefully revised. The changes he made in his text were not, however, substantive; he sought rather to "point up" the prose, to create a richer verbal texture, to give the edition a uniform polish and maturity. At times old simplicities were sacrificed to the over-ornate; nevertheless the revisions invariably result in more explicit statement.

To each novel, and each collection of tales, James affixed a long and tightly written preface — again after the manner of Balzac. These are of a piece with the novelist's critical writings — the reviews, portraits, and essays he had written for periodicals and newspapers during his entire career. His criticism had reflected from the first the clearly formulated canons of his novelist's art.

37

The collections he put forth himself during his lifetime testify to this — *French Poets and Novelists, Partial Portraits, Essays in London,* and *Notes on Novelists.* As a critic, James is eclectic and classical in his mode of thought: he insists upon form, on style, on integration of form and substance. He unerringly selects the very writers we today consider to have been "major" in his time; and he reads them for what they may teach him of his own process, and for the "quality of mind" he may find in their work. He believes that the artist is to be discovered in his work; but that the work must be created as an "invulnerable granite" to the seeker.

The late prefaces, since collected in a single volume, are composed of three elements: there is the author's interest in his creative process, the "story of the story," how he came to write it and the personal memories and associations aroused by the rereading of his own work; there is the discussion of the technical problems involved in each case; and, with all this, there are James's generalizations on the art of novel writing which form the heart of these essays and give them remarkable force as critical documents. The pages are crowded with critical ideas; they show the creative and analytical vision of an artist who meditates on his career and on old artistic problems long since resolved in his workshop. He felt, as he wrote the prefaces, that they would someday be a great manifesto on the art of the novel and would serve as a guide for writers of fiction. His belief was well founded; the prefaces gave to criticism for the first time a valuable terminology for the discussion of the novel. To be sure, the craft of novel writing had been discussed on many occasions during the nineteenth century, but James, in some measure, codified this discussion in these last and most personal of his critical essays, gave it system and authority in the light of his half century of practice.

Although he wrote no more novels, James's productivity during his final years was remarkable. Following the pattern of the New

York Edition, he revised his travel writings and consolidated them; thus *English Hours* appeared, and then *Italian Hours* which, with his *Little Tour in France*, commemorated the pathways James had taken during his lifetime on the Continent. He issued a final collection of essays on the eve of the war, *Notes on Novelists*, containing magisterial studies of Flaubert, Zola, and Balzac and his protest against the forms naturalism had taken in the new English novel, particularly as exemplified in the realistic fiction of H. G. Wells and Arnold Bennett. In addition he wrote two remarkable volumes of reminiscence — *A Small Boy and Others* and *Notes of a Son and Brother*, looking back at his own past with the same search for the truths of the emotions which Proust was to show in his novel *A la recherche du temps perdu*. His *Notes* embodied also his memories of his brother William, who had recently died, and those of his father. A third volume of reminiscence, destined to deal with his years in London and Paris, was left a mere fragment, and was published as *The Middle Years* after James's death.

The English-speaking world honored him on his seventieth birthday; and while efforts to obtain the Nobel Prize for him failed, James was given a golden bowl by 250 friends and admirers who also asked him to sit for his portrait to John Singer Sargent. That portrait is now in the National Portrait Gallery in London.

With the outbreak of the war James threw himself into various activities: he visited hospitals, aided refugees, and wrote on behalf of the American volunteer motor ambulance corps in France. Ill and suffering, he decided in 1915 to yield the American citizenship he had retained during his forty years' residence in England, and throw in his lot with the British cause. A stroke three or four months later was followed by pneumonia, and although he survived into 1916, and was given the Order of Merit by King George V, it was clear that there would be no recovery. He died on February 28. His ashes were brought to America and interred in the family plot in Cambridge. An inscription on his grave describes him as the interpreter of his generation on both sides of the sea.

At first, after James's death, there was a period during which his works were dismissed as thin and lifeless by a generation that had read only a few of his books and had lost sight of the total structure of his literary edifice. For a decade or more the view put forth by Van Wyck Brooks, that James, in uprooting himself from his native land, had produced a rootless art, prevailed. Moreover the publication of James's letters in 1920 tended to establish for posterity the "Old Pretender" James, the heavy long-winded figure of Rye and Chelsea, rather than the robust bearded creative James of the turn of the century. This was due to the fact that much of the earlier correspondence was not available to Percy Lubbock, the editor of the letters, who in particular did not have James's "working" letters, his correspondence with editors and publishers; he assembled two volumes which show James the social being and "theorist" of fiction, but not the Balzacian "professional."

The only posthumous works published were the two unfinished novels, *The Sense of the Past* and *The Ivory Tower*, and the fragment of autobiography, *The Middle Years*. James's other papers were allowed to remain in the trunk in which they had been packed and sent back to America. They ultimately passed into the possession of Harvard University, at the time of the James centenary in 1943, when it became clear that there was still much of James to be given to the world. Most important of all were certain of his working notebooks, which when published in 1947 showed the source material out of which the prefaces had been written. These notebooks constitute one of the most remarkable records of an artist-life ever preserved. Written often in the full blaze of creation, they demonstrate James's way of reimagining his materials and the strange, often calculating intellectual force he brought to bear upon his work.

James had been a constant letter-writer from the first. His letters are the surplus production of a writer who, having done his day's work, is unable to stop, and writes on with a free flow and an easy play of imagination. More than ten thousand letters survive, the majority unpublished, and his professional letters, no less than those written in friendship, are filled with remarkable observation of the people and places of his time.

His friendships were numerous. He moved everywhere in the literary and art world and crossed the path of nearly all the leading writers of his day. He knew more intimately among writers, critics, painters, Robert Browning, Robert Louis Stevenson, Edmund Gosse, Alphonse Daudet, Ivan Turgenev, Paul Bourget, George du Maurier, John Singer Sargent, John La Farge, Émile Zola, Jules Jusserand, Mrs. Humphry Ward and later Joseph Conrad, H. G. Wells, Rudyard Kipling, Edith Wharton. He had met Matthew Arnold in Rome and later in London, chatted in London drawing rooms with Pater, and had encountered Tennyson and George Eliot, William Morris and John Ruskin. If we add the earlier friendship with Emerson, and his close ties with Norton and Howells, it can be seen that James was far from being the recluse of Rye, as he has sometimes been pictured. He touched his age largely during his half-century in the creative world. He tends increasingly to dominate the literature of America because the ramifications of his career are considerable — and complex — beside the simpler lives and simpler works of other American novelists. The so-called "revival" of James has in reality been the discovery of him as a great world literary figure, a veritable bridge from the romantic movement to all that is "modern" in the literary art of the twentieth century.

↗ Selected Bibliography

FOR a complete listing of Henry James's writings see *A Bibliography of Henry James* by Leon Edel and Dan H. Laurence (London: Hart-Davis, 1957) which establishes the priority of editions as between America and England, and also lists foreign translations of James's writings. Much of James is out of print; and the rather considerable reprinting of him in recent years has tended to be haphazard with repetition of well-known titles. The present selection lists his books under the titles they bore on original appearance and gives first place of publication.

Collected Editions

Collected Novels and Tales. 14 volumes. London: Macmillan, 1883.
The Novels and Tales of Henry James ("New York Edition"). 24 volumes. New York: Scribner's, 1907–9. (Two volumes were added posthumously.)
Uniform Edition of the Tales. 14 volumes. London: Secker, 1915–19. (There was one tale in each volume — that is, 14 tales in all were published, of the more than 100 written by James.)
The Novels and Stories of Henry James. 36 volumes. London: Macmillan, 1921–23.

Novels

Roderick Hudson. Boston: Osgood, 1875.
The American. Boston: Osgood, 1877.
Watch and Ward. Boston: Houghton, Osgood, 1878.
The Europeans. London: Macmillan, 1878.
Confidence. London: Chatto and Windus, 1879.
Washington Square. New York: Harper, 1881 [1880].
The Portrait of a Lady. London: Macmillan, 1881.
The Bostonians. London: Macmillan, 1886.
The Princess Casamassima. London: Macmillan, 1886.
The Tragic Muse. Boston: Houghton, Mifflin, 1889.
The Other House. London: Heinemann, 1896.
The Spoils of Poynton. London: Heinemann, 1897.
What Maisie Knew. London: Heinemann, 1897.

42

The Awkward Age. London: Heinemann, 1899.
The Sacred Fount. New York: Scribner's, 1901.
The Wings of the Dove. New York: Scribner's, 1902.
The Ambassadors. London: Methuen, 1903.
The Golden Bowl. New York: Scribner's, 1904.
The Outcry. London: Methuen, 1911.

Posthumous Novels

The Ivory Tower. London: Collins, 1917. (Uncompleted.)
The Sense of the Past. London: Collins, 1917. (Uncompleted.)

Tales

TITLES marked with an asterisk are special titles assigned by James to books containing his tales. All other titles are actual tale titles, often used as title of the book. Where the title is not italicized, the tale was published alone.

A Passionate Pilgrim and Other Tales. Boston: Osgood, 1875.
"Daisy Miller." New York: Harper, 1879 [1878].
"An International Episode." New York: Harper, 1879.
The Madonna of the Future and Other Tales. London: Macmillan, 1879.
"The Diary of a Man of Fifty." New York: Harper, 1880.
The Siege of London and Other Tales. Boston: Osgood, 1883.
Tales of Three Cities. Boston: Osgood, 1884.
The Author of Beltraffio and Other Tales. Boston: Osgood, 1885.
Stories Revived. 3 volumes. London: Macmillan, 1885.
The Reverberator. London: Macmillan, 1888.
The Aspern Papers. London: Macmillan, 1888.
A London Life. London: Macmillan, 1889.
The Lesson of the Master. New York: Macmillan, 1892.
The Real Thing and Other Tales. New York: Macmillan, 1893.
The Private Life. London: Osgood, McIlvaine, 1893.
The Wheel of Time. New York: Harper, 1893.
* *Terminations.* London: Heinemann, 1895.
* *Embarrassments.* London: Heinemann, 1896.
In the Cage. London: Duckworth, 1898.
* *The Two Magics.* London: Heinemann, 1898.
* *The Soft Side.* London: Methuen, 1900.
* *The Better Sort.* London: Methuen, 1903 .
"Julia Bride." New York: Harper, 1909.
* *The Finer Grain.* New York: Scribner's, 1910.

Posthumous Collections of Tales

"Gabrielle de Bergerac." New York: Boni and Liveright, 1918.

Travelling Companions, edited by Albert Mordell. New York: Boni and Liveright, 1919.

A Landscape Painter, edited by Albert Mordell. New York: Scott and Seltzer, 1919 [1920].

Master Eustace, edited by Albert Mordell. New York: Seltzer, 1920.

The American Novels and Stories, edited by F. O. Matthiessen. New York: Knopf, 1948.

The Ghostly Tales of Henry James, edited by Leon Edel. New Brunswick, N.J.: Rutgers University Press, 1948 [1949].

Eight Uncollected Tales, edited by Edna Kenton. New Brunswick, N.J.: Rutgers University Press, 1950.

Autobiographies

William Wetmore Story and His Friends. Edinburgh: Blackwood, 1903. (Biographical memoir.)

A Small Boy and Others. New York: Scribner's, 1913.

Notes of a Son and Brother. New York: Scribner's, 1914.

The Middle Years. London: Collins, 1917. (Uncompleted.)

Letters

The Letters of Henry James, edited by Percy Lubbock. 2 volumes. London: Macmillan, 1920.

Letters of Henry James to A. C. Benson. New York: Scribner's, 1930.

Theatre and Friendship. London: Cape, 1932. (Letters of James to Elizabeth Robins.)

Henry James and Robert Louis Stevenson, edited by Janet A. Smith. London: Hart-Davis, 1948.

Selected Letters of Henry James, edited by Leon Edel. New York: Farrar, Straus, 1955.

Henry James and H. G. Wells, edited by Leon Edel and Gordon N. Ray. London: Hart-Davis, 1958.

Plays

Daisy Miller, A Comedy. Boston: Osgood, 1883.

Theatricals. London: Osgood, McIlvaine, 1894.

Theatricals; Second Series. London: Osgood, McIlvaine, 1894.

The Complete Plays of Henry James, edited by Leon Edel. Philadelphia: Lippincott, 1949.

Essays, Criticism, and Miscellaneous Writings

French Poets and Novelists. London: Macmillan, 1878.
Hawthorne. London: Macmillan, 1879.
Partial Portraits. London: Macmillan, 1888.
Essays in London and Elsewhere. London: Osgood, McIlvaine, 1893.
Picture and Text. New York: Harper, 1893.
The Question of Our Speech. Boston: Houghton, Mifflin, 1905.
Views and Reviews, collected by Le Roy Phillips. Boston: Ball, 1908.
Notes on Novelists. London: Dent, 1914.

Posthumous Collections of Essays, Criticism, and Miscellaneous Writings

Within the Rim. London: Collins, 1919.
Notes and Reviews, edited by Pierre la Rose. Cambridge, Mass.: Dunster House, 1921.
The Art of the Novel, edited by R. P. Blackmur. New York: Scribner's, 1934.
The Notebooks of Henry James, edited by F. O. Matthiessen and Kenneth B. Murdock. New York: Oxford University Press, 1947.
The Scenic Art, edited by Allan Wade. New Brunswick, N.J.: Rutgers University Press, 1948.
The American Essays of Henry James, edited by Leon Edel. New York: Knopf (Vintage), 1956.
The Future of the Novel, edited by Leon Edel. New York: Knopf (Vintage), 1956.
The Painter's Eye, edited by John L. Sweeney. London: Hart-Davis, 1956.
The House of Fiction, edited by Leon Edel. London: Hart-Davis, 1957.
Literary Reviews and Essays, edited by Albert Mordell. New York: Grove, 1957.

Travel

Transatlantic Sketches. Boston: Osgood, 1875. (Titled *Foreign Parts* in Tauchnitz Edition, 1884.)
Portraits of Places. London: Macmillan, 1883.
A Little Tour in France. Boston: Osgood, 1885 [1884].
English Hours. London: Heinemann, 1905.
The American Scene. London: Chapman and Hall, 1907.
Italian Hours. London: Heinemann, 1909.

LEON EDEL

Posthumous Travel Collections

Parisian Sketches, edited by Leon Edel and Ilse Lind. New York: New York University Press, 1957.
The Art of Travel, edited by Morton D. Zabel. New York: Doubleday, 1958.

Current American Reprints

The Ambassadors. New York: Anchor Books (Doubleday). $1.25. New York: Harper's Modern Classics $1.25. Greenwich, Conn.: Premier (Fawcett Publications). $.50. Boston: Riverside (Houghton Mifflin). Forthcoming. New York: Signet (New American Library). $.50.

The American. New York: Dell. $.50. New York: Rinehart Reprint Series. $1.75.

The Art of the Novel. New York: Scribner Library. $1.45.

The Aspern Papers and the Spoils of Poynton. New York: Dell. $.50.

The Awkward Age. New York: Anchor Books. $1.25.

The Bostonians. New York: Modern Library (Random House). $1.95.

The Golden Bowl. New York: Evergreen (Grove). $1.95.

In the Cage. New York: Anchor Books. $1.25.

Italian Hours. New York: Evergreen. $1.95.

The Portable Henry James, edited by Morton D. Zabel. New York: Viking. $1.45.

The Portrait of a Lady. New York: Modern Library. $1.95. Boston: Riverside. $.90.

The Princess Casamassima. New York: Torchbooks (Harper). $1.85.

The Reverberator. New York: Evergreen. $1.45.

Roderick Hudson. New York: Torchbooks. $1.60.

The Sacred Fount. New York: Evergreen. $1.45.

Scenic Art, edited by Allan Wade. New York: Dramabooks (Hill and Wang). $1.35.

Selected Fiction, edited by Leon Edel. New York: Everyman (Dutton). $2.45.

Selected Short Stories, edited by Quentin Anderson. New York: Rinehart Reprint Series. $.95.

Short Stories (selected), edited by Clifton Fadiman. New York: Modern Library. $2.95.

The Tragic Muse. New York: Torchbooks. $2.25.

The Turn of the Screw and Daisy Miller. New York: Dell. $.35.

Washington Square. New York: Bantam. $.35. New York: Modern Library. $1.95.

Watch and Ward. New York: Evergreen. $1.95.

What Maisie Knew. New York: Anchor Books. $.85.

46

The Wings of the Dove. New York: Dell. $.50. New York: Modern Library. $1.95.

Biographical and Critical Studies

Beach, Joseph Warren. *The Method of Henry James.* New Haven, Conn.: Yale University Press, 1918.

Brooks, Van Wyck. *The Pilgrimage of Henry James.* New York: Dutton, 1925.

Dupee, F. W. *Henry James.* New York: Sloane, 1951.

————, ed. *The Question of Henry James.* New York: Holt, 1945.

Edel, Leon. *Henry James: The Untried Years.* Philadelphia: Lippincott, 1953.

Grattan, C. H. *The Three Jameses.* New York: Longmans, Green, 1932.

Lubbock, Percy. *The Craft of Fiction.* New York: Scribner's, 1921.

Matthiessen, F. O. *Henry James: The Major Phase.* New York: Oxford University Press, 1944.

————. *The James Family.* New York: Knopf, 1947.

Nowell-Smith, Simon, ed. *The Legend of the Master.* London: Constable, 1948 [1947].

Wilson, Edmund. *The Triple Thinkers.* New York: Harcourt, Brace, 1938.